Encyclopedia of
SPECIAL
EDUCATION
Second Edition

Encyclopedia of Special Education, SECOND EDITION
Cecil R. Reynolds and Elaine Fletcher-Janzen, Editors

Encyclopedia of
SPECIAL
EDUCATION

Second Edition

A Reference for the Education of the Handicapped and Other Exceptional Children and Adults

VOLUME 1

Edited by

Cecil R. Reynolds
Texas A & M University

Elaine Fletcher-Janzen
University of Northern Colorado

JOHN WILEY & SONS

NEW YORK · CHICHESTER · WEINHEIM · BRISBANE · SINGAPORE · TORONTO

ISBN 0-471-25323-5 (Volume 1)
ISBN 0-471-25324-3 (Volume 2)
ISBN 0-471-25325-1 (Volume 3)
ISBN 0-471-25309-X (three-volume set)

Printed in the United States of America.

10 9 8 7 6 5 4 3 2 1

CONTRIBUTORS

Susanne Blough Abbott
Bedford Central School District
Mt. Kisco, New York

Marty Abramson
University of Wisconsin at Stout
Menomonie, Wisconsin

Patricia Ann Abramson
Hudson Public Schools
Hudson, Wisconsin

Salvador Hector Achoa
Texas A & M University
College Station, Texas

Patricia A. Alexander
University of Maryland
College Park, Maryland

Nancy Algert
Texas A & M University
College Station, Texas

Thomas E. Allen
Gallaudet College
Washington, DC

Marie Almond
The University of Texas of the
  Permian Basin
Odessa, Texas

Geri R. Alvis
University of Tennessee
Memphis State University
Memphis, Tennessee

C.H. Ammons
Psychological Reports/
  Perceptual and Motor Skills
Missoula, Montana

Carol Anderson
Texas A & M University
College Station, Texas

Kari Anderson
University of North Carolina
Wilmington, North Carolina

Peggy L. Anderson
University of New Orleans,
  Lakefront
New Orleans, Louisiana

J. Appelboom-Fondu
Université Libre de Bruxelles
Brussels, Belgium

James M. Applefield
University of North Carolina
Wilmington, North Carolina

Pauline F. Applefield
University of North Carolina
Wilmington, North Carolina

John Arena
Academic Therapy Publications
Novato, California

Kim Ryan Arredondo
Texas A & M University
College Station, Texas

Gustavo Abelardo Arrendondo
Monterrey, Mexico

Bernice Arricale
Hunter College, City University
  of New York
New York, New York

H. Roberta Arrigo
Hunter College, City University
  of New York
New York, New York

Alfredo J. Artiles
University of California
Los Angeles, California

Michael J. Ash
Texas A & M University
College Station, Texas

Adel E. Ashawal
Ain Shams University
Cairo, Egypt

William G. Austin
Cape Fear Psychological Services
Wilmington, North Carolina

Anna H. Avant
University of Alabama
University, Alabama

Dan G. Bachor
University of Victoria
Canada

Rebecca Bailey
Texas A & M University
College Station, Texas

Timothy A. Ballard
University of North Carolina
Wilmington, North Carolina

Deborah E. Barbour
University of North Carolina
Wilmington, North Carolina

Russell A. Barkley
University of Massachusetts
  Medical Center
Worchester, Massachusetts

Charles P. Barnard
University of Wisconsin at Stout
Menomonie, Wisconsin

David W. Barnett
University of Cincinnati
Cincinnati, Ohio

Ellis I. Barowsky
Hunter College, City University
  of New York
New York, New York

Lyle E. Barton
Kent State University
Kent, Ohio

Vicki Bartosik
Stanford University
Stanford, California

Paul Bates
Southern Illinois University
Carbondale, Illinois

Anne M. Bauer
University of Cincinnati
Cincinnati, Ohio

Elizabeth R. Bauerschmidt
University of North Carolina
Wilmington, North Carolina

Michael Bauerschmidt
Brunswick Hospital
Wilmington, North Carolina

Monique Bauters
Centre d'Etude et de Reclassement
Brussels, Belgium

John R. Beattie
University of North Carolina
Charlotte, North Carolina

George R. Beauchamp
Cleveland Clinic Foundation
Cleveland, Ohio

Ana Yeraldina Beneke
University of Oklahoma
Norman, Oklahoma

Randy Elliot Bennett
Educational Testing Service
Princeton, New Jersey

Richard A. Berg
West Virginia University Medical
  Center, Charleston Division
Charleston, West Virginia

John R. Bergan
University of Arizona
Tucson, Arizona

Dianne E. Berkell
C.W. Post Campus, Long Island
  University
Greenvale, New York

Gary Berkowitz
Temple University
Philadelphia, Pennsylvania

Shari A. Stanton
Private Practice
Las Vegas, Nevada

Kristen Biernath
The Hughes Spalding International
  Adoption Evaluation Center
Georgia

Erin D. Bigler
Austin Neurological Clinic
University of Texas
Austin, Texas

Roseann Bisighini
The Salk Institute
La Jolla, California

L. Worth Bolton
Cape Fear Substance Abuse Center
Wilmington, North Carolina

Gwyneth M. Boodoo
Texas A & M University
College Station, Texas

Nancy Bordier
Hunter College, City University
  of New York
New York, New York

Jeannie Bormans
Center for Developmental Problems
Brussels, Belgium

Morton Botel
University of Pennsylvania
Philadelphia, Pennsylvania

Daniel J. Boudah
Texas A & M University
College Station, Texas

Michael Bourdot
Centre d'Etude et de Reclassement
Brussels, Belgium

Bruce A. Bracken
University of Memphis
Memphis, Tennessee

Mary Brady
Pennsylvania Special Education
  Assistive Device Center
Elizabethtown, Pennsylvania

Janet S. Brand
Hunter College, City University
  of New York
New York, New York

Don Braswell
Research Foundation, City
  University of New York
New York, New York

T. Berry Brazelton
Children's Hospital
Boston, Massachusetts

Warner H. Britton
Auburn University
Auburn, Alabama

Debra Y. Broadbooks
California School of
  Professional Psychology
San Diego, California

Michael G. Brown
Central Wisconsin Center for the
  Developmentally Disabled
Madison, Wisconsin

Robert T. Brown
University of North Carolina
Wilmington, North Carolina

Ronald T. Brown
Emory University School
  of Medicine
Atlanta, Georgia

Tina L. Brown
University of Tennessee
Memphis State University
Memphis, Tennessee

Robert G. Brubaker
Eastern Kentucky University
Richmond, Kentucky

Catherine O. Bruce
Hunter College, City University
  of New York
New York, New York

Andrew R. Brulle
Eastern Illinois University
Charleston, Illinois

Laura Kinzie Brutting
University of Wisconsin
Madison, Wisconsin

Donna M. Bryant
University of North Carolina
Chapel Hill, North Carolina

Milton Budoff
Research Institute for
  Educational Problems
Cambridge, Massachusetts

Carolyn Bullard
Lewis & Clark College
Portland, Oregon

Thomas Burke
Hunter College, City University
  of New York
New York, New York

Alois Bürli
Swiss Institute for Special Education
Lucerne, Switzerland

Thomas A. Burton
University of Georgia
Athens, GA

James Button
United States Department
  of Education
Washington, DC

Anne Campbell
Purdue University
West Lafayette, Indiana

Frances A. Campbell
University of North Carolina
Chapel Hill, North Carolina

Steven A. Carlson
Beaverton Schools
Beaverton, Oregon

Douglas Carnine
University of Oregon
Eugene, Oregon

Janet Carpenter
University of Oklahoma
Norman, Oklahoma

Tracy Calpin Castle
Eastern Kentucky University
Richmond, Kentucky

John F. Cawley
University of New Orleans
New Orleans, Louisiana

Constance Y. Celaya
Private Practice
Irving, Texas

James C. Chalfant
University of Arizona
Tucson, Arizona

Chris Cherrington
Lycoming College
Williamsport, Pennsylvania

Robert Chimedza
University of Zimbabwe
Havare, Zimbabwe

Kathleen Chinn
New Mexico State University
Las Cruces, New Mexico

LeRoy Clinton
Boston University
Boston, Massachusetts

Renato Cocchi
Pesaro, Italy

Shirley Cohen
Hunter College, City University
  of New York
New York, New York

Ginga L. Colcough
University of North Carolina
Wilmington, North Carolina

Christine L. Cole
University of Wisconsin
Madison, Wisconsin

Rhonda Collins
Florida State University
Tallahassee, Florida

Jennifer Condon
University of North Carolina
Wilmington, North Carolina

Jane Close Conoley
University of Nebraska
Lincoln, Nebraska

Vivian I. Correa
University of Florida
Gainesville, Florida

Lawrence S. Cote
Pennsylvania State University
University Park, Pennsylvania

Katherine D. Couturier
Pennsylvania State University
King of Prussia, Pennsylvania

J. Michael Coxe
University of South Carolina
Columbia, South Carolina

Anne B. Crabbe
St. Andrews College
Laurinburg, North Carolina

Sergio R. Crisalle
Medical Horizons Unlimited
San Antonio, Texas

Chara Crivelli
Vito de Negrar
Verona, Italy

Jack A. Cummings
Indiana University
Bloomington, Indiana

Jacqueline Cunningham
University of Texas
Austin, Texas

Susan Curtiss
University of California
Los Angeles, California

Rik Carl D'Amato
University of Northern Colorado
Greely, Colorado

CONTRIBUTORS

Elizabeth Dane
Hunter College, City University
   of New York
New York, New York

Craig Darch
Auburn University
Auburn, Alabama

Jacqueline E. Davis
Boston University
Boston, Massachusetts

Raymond S. Dean
Ball State University
Indiana University School
   of Medicine
Muncie, Indiana

Jozi Deleon
New Mexico State University
Las Cruces, New Mexico

Bernadette M. Delgado
Puerto Rico

Randall L. De Pry
University of Colorado
Colorado Springs, Colorado

Lizanne DeStefano
University of Illinois,
   Urbana-Champaign
Champaign, Illinois

S. De Vriendt
Vrije Universiteit Brussel
Brussels, Belgium

Caroline D'Ippolito
Eastern Pennsylvania Special
   Education Resources Center
King of Prussia, Pennsylvania

Mary D'Ippolito
Montgomery County
   Intermediate Unit
Norristown, Pennsylvania

Marilyn P. Dornbush
Atlanta, Georgia

Susann Dowling
University of North Carolina
Wilmington, North Carolina

Jengjyh Duh
National Taiwan Normal University
Taiwan

Brooke Durbin
Texas A & M University
College Station, Texas

Mary K. Dykes
University of Florida
Gainesville, Florida

Peg Eagney
School for the Deaf
New York, New York

Ronald C. Eaves
Auburn University
Auburn, Alabama

Jana Echevarria
California State University
Long Beach, California

Amita Edran
California State University
Long Beach, California

John M. Eells
Souderton Area School District
Souderton, Pennsylvania

Stephen N. Elliott
University of Wisconsin
Madison, Wisconsin

Ingemar Emanuelsson
Goteburg University
Sweden

Carol Sue Englert
Michigan State University
East Lansing, Michigan

Christine A. Espin
University of Minnesota
Minneapolis, Minnesota

Rand B. Evans
Texas A & M University
College Station, Texas

Katherine Falwell
University of North Carolina
Wilmington, North Carolina

Stephen S. Farmer
New Mexico State University
Las Cruces, New Mexico

MaryAnn C. Farthing
University of North Carolina
Chapel Hill, North Carolina

Lisa Fashnacht Hill
California School of
   Professional Psychology
San Diego, California

Mary Grace Feely
School for the Deaf
New York, New York

John F. Feldhusen
Purdue University
West Lafayette, Indiana

Britt-Inger Fex
University of Lund
Sweden

Donna Filips
Steger, Illinois

Sally L. Flagler
University of Oklahoma
Norman, Oklahoma

Dennis M. Flanagan
Montgomery County
   Intermediate Unit
Norristown, Pennsylvania

David Fletcher-Janzen
Colorado Springs, Colorado

Elaine Fletcher-Janzen
University of Northern Colorado
Colorado Springs, Colorado

Wendy Flynn
Staffordshire University
England

Thomas A. Frank
Pennsylvania State University
University Park, Pennsylvania

Mary M. Frasier
University of Georgia
Athens, Georgia

Joseph L. French
Pennsylvania State University
University Park, Pennsylvania

Alice G. Friedman
University of Oklahoma Health
    Services Center
Norman, Oklahoma

Douglas L. Friedman
Fordham University
Bronx, New York

Douglas Fuchs
Peabody College, Vanderbilt
    University
Nashville, Tennessee

Lynn S. Fuchs
Peabody College, Vanderbilt
    University
Nashville, Tennessee

Gerald B. Fuller
Central Michigan University
Mt. Pleasant, Michigan

Rosemary Gaffney
Hunter College, City University
    of New York
New York, New York

Diego Gallegos
Texas A & M University
College Station, Texas
San Antonio Independent
    School District
San Antonio, Texas

Shernaz B. Garcia
University of Texas
Austin, Texas

Katherine Garnett
Hunter College, City University
    of New York
New York, New York

Melissa M. George
Montgomery County
    Intermediate Unit
Norristown, Pennsylvania

Phil Bless Gerard
University of Fribourg
Switzerland

Harvey R. Gilbert
Pennsylvania State University
University Park, Pennsylvania

Elizabeth Girshick
Montgomery County
    Intermediate Unit
Norristown, Pennsylvania

Joni J. Gleason
University of West Florida
Pensacola, Florida

Sharon L. Glennen
Pennsylvania State University
University Park, Pennsylvania

Rick Gonzales
Texas A & M University
College Station, Texas

Libby Goodman
Pennsylvania State University
King of Prussia, Pennsylvania

Carole Reiter Gothelf
Hunter College, City University
    of New York
New York, New York

Steve Graham
University of Maryland
College Park, Maryland

Jeffrey W. Gray
Ball State University
Muncie, Indiana

P. Allen Gray, Jr.
University North Carolina
Wilmington, North Carolina

Darielle Greenberg
California School of
    Professional Psychology
San Diego, California

Laurence C. Grimm
University of Illinois
Chicago, Illinois

Lindsay S. Gross
University of Wisconsin
Milwaukee, Wisconsin

Norma Guerra
Texas A & M University
College Station, Texas

John Guidubaldi
Kent State University
Kent, Ohio

Deborah Guillen
The University of Texas of the
    Permian Basin
Odessa, Texas

Steven Gumerman
Temple University
Philadelphia, Pennsylvania

Thomas Gumpel
The Hebrew University of Jerusalem
Israel

Terry B. Gutkin
University of Nebraska
Lincoln, Nebraska

Patricia A. Haensly
Texas A & M University
College Station, Texas

George James Hagerty
Stonehill College
North Easton, Massachusetts

Robert Hall
Texas A & M University
College Station, Texas

Winnifred M. Hall
University of West Indies
Jamaica

Richard E. Halmstad
University of Wisconsin at Stout
Menomonie, Wisconsin

Glennelle Halpin
Auburn University
Auburn, Alabama

Donald D. Hammill
Pro-Ed, Inc.
Austin, Texas

Harold Hanson
Southern Illinois University
Carbondale, Illinois

Elise Phelps Hanzel
California School of
    Professional Psychology
San Diego, California

Janice Harper
North Carolina Central University
Durham, North Carolina

Gale A. Harr
Maple Heights City Schools
Maple Heights, Ohio

Karen L. Harrell
University of Georgia
Athens, Georgia

Frances T. Harrington
Radford University
Blacksberg, Virginia

Karen R. Harris
University of Maryland
College Park, Maryland

Kathleen Harris
Arizona State University West
Arizona

Patti L. Harrison
University of Alabama
University, Alabama

Beth Harry
University of Miami
Miami, Florida

Lawrence C. Hartlage
Evans, Georgia

Patricia Hartlage
Medical College of Georgia
Evans, Georgia

Dan Hatt
University of Oklahoma
Norman, Oklahoma

Anette Hausotter
Bis Beratungsstelle Fur Die
    Intergration
Germany

Jeff Heinzen
Indianhead Enterprise
Menomonie, Wisconsin

Rhonda Hennis
University of North Carolina
Wilmington, North Carolina

Arthur Hernandez
Texas A & M University
College Station, Texas

E. Valerie Hewitt
Texas A & M University
College Station, Texas

Julia A. Hickman
Bastrop Mental Health Association
Bastrop, Texas

Craig S. Higgins
Stonehill College
North Easton, Massachusetts

Alan Hilton
Seattle University
Seattle, Washington

Delores J. Hittinger
The University of Texas of the
    Permian Basin
Odessa, Texas

Harold E. Hoff, Jr.
Eastern Pennsylvania Special
    Education
    Resources Center
King of Prussia, Pennsylvania

Elizabeth Holcomb
American Journal of
    Occupational Therapy
Bethesda, Maryland

E. Wayne Holden
University of Oklahoma Health
    Sciences Center
Norman, Ohlahoma

Ivan Z. Holowinsky
Rutgers University
New Brunswick, New Jersey

Thomas F. Hopkins
Center for Behavioral Psychotherapy
White Plains, New York

Wayne P. Hresko
Journal of Learning Disabilities
Austin, Texas

Charles A. Hughes
Pennsylvania State University
University Park, Pennsylvania

Jan N. Hughes
Texas A & M University
College Station, Texas

Kay E. Hughes
The Riverside Publishing Company
Itasca, Illinois

Aimee Hunter
University of North Carolina
Wilmington, North Carolina

Nancy L. Hutchinson
Simon Fraser University
Buraby, British Columbia

Beverly J. Irby
Sam Houston State University
Texas

Paul Irvine
Katonah, New York

Lee Anderson Jackson, Jr.
University of North Carolina
Wilmington, North Carolina

Markku Jahnukainen
University of Helsinki
Finland

Diane Jarvis
State University of New York
Buffalo, New York

Phillip Jenkins
University of Kentucky
Lexington, Kentucky

Elizabeth Jones
Texas A & M University
College Station, Texas

Gideon Jones
Florida State University
Tallahassee, Florida

Philip R. Jones
Virginia Polytechnic Institute
    and State University
Blacksburg, Virginia

Shirley A. Jones
Virginia Polytechnic Institute
    and State University
Blacksburg, Virginia

James W. Kalat
North Carolina State University
Raleigh, North Carolina

Maya Kalyanpur
Towson University
Towson, Maryland

Randy W. Kamphaus
University of Georgia
Athens, Georgia

Harrison Kane
University of Florida
Gainesville, Florida

Stan A. Karcz
University of Wisconsin at Stout
Menomonie, Wisconsin

Maribeth Montgomery Kasik
Governors State University
University Park, Illinois

Alan S. Kaufman
Yale University School of Medicine
New Haven, Connecticut

James Kaufman
Yale University
New Haven, Connecticut

Nancy J. Kaufman
University of Wisconsin
Stevens Point, Wisconsin

Kenneth A. Kavale
University of Iowa
Iowa City, Iowa

Hortencia Kayser
New Mexico State University
Las Cruces, New Mexico

Forrest E. Keesbury
Lycoming College
Williamsport, Pennsylvania

Barbara Keogh
University of California
Los Angeles, California

Kay E. Ketzenberger
The University of Texas of the
    Permian Basin
Odessa, Texas

Peggy Kipling
Pro-Ed, Inc.
Austin, Texas

Gonul Kircaali-Iftar
Anadolu University
Turkey

Margie K. Kitano
New Mexico State University
Las Cruces, New Mexico

F. J. Koopmans-Van Beinum
Amsterdam, The Netherlands

Mark A. Koorland
Florida State University
Tallahassee, Florida

L. Koulischer
Institut de Morphologie Pathologique
Belgium

Martin Kozloff
University of North Carolina
Wilmington, North Carolina

Howard M. Knoff
University of South Florida
Tampa, Florida

Thomas R. Kratochwill
University of Wisconsin
Madison, Wisconsin

James P. Krouse
Clarion University of Pennsylvania
Clarion, Pennsylvania

Louis J. Kruger
Tufts University
Medford, Pennsylvania

Timothy D. Lackaye
Hunter College, City University
    of New York
New York, New York

C. Sue Lamb
University of North Carolina
Wilmington, North Carolina

Nadine M. Lambert
University of California
Berkeley, California

Louis J. LaNunziata
University of North Carolina
Wilmington, North Carolina

Rafael Lara-Alecio
Texas A & M University
College Station, Texas

Franco Larocca
The University of Verona
Italy

Jeff Laurent
University of Texas
Austin, Texas

Samuel LeBaron
University of Texas Health
    Science Center
San Antonio, Texas

Yvan Lebrun
School of Medicine
Brussels, Belgium

Linda Leeper
New Mexico State University
Las Cruces, New Mexico

Ronald S. Lenkowsky
Hunter College, City University
    of New York
New York, New York

Mary Louise Lennon
Educational Testing Service
Princeton, New Jersey

Richard Levak
California School of
    Professional Psychology
San Diego, California

Allison Lewis
University of North Carolina
Wilmington, North Carolina

Collette Leyva
Texas A & M University
College Station, Texas

Elizabeth Lichtenberger
The Salk Institute
La Jolla, California

Ping Lin
Elmhurst College
Elmhurst, Illinois

Ken Linfoot
University of Western Sydney
Australia

Janet A. Lindow
University of Wisconsin
Madison, Wisconsin

Daniel D. Lipka
Lincoln Way Special Education
  Regional Resources Center
Louisville, Ohio

Cornelia Lively
University of Illinois,
  Urbana-Champaign
Champaign, Illinois

Jeri Logemann
Northwestern University
Evanston, Illinois

Charles J. Long
University of Memphis
Memphis, Tennessee

Linda R. Longley
University of North Carolina
Wilmington, North Carolina

Emilia C. Lopez
Fordham University
New York, New York

Patricia Lowe
Texas A & M University
College Station, Texas

Marsha H. Lupi
Hunter College, City University
  of New York
New York, New York

Ann E. Lupkowski
Texas A & M University
College Station, Texas

Pat Lynch
Texas A & M University
College Station, Texas

Philip E. Lyon
College of St. Rose
Albany, New York

Charles A. MacArthur
University of Maryland
College Park, Maryland

John MacDonald
Eastern Kentucky University
Richmond, Kentucky

Taddy Maddox
Pro Ed, Inc.
Austin, Texas

Ghislain Magerotte
Mons State University
Mons, Belgium

Susan Mahanna-Boden
Eastern Kentucky University
Richmond, Kentucky

Charles A. Maher
Rutgers University
Piscataway, New Jersey

Elba Maldonado-Colon
San Jose State University
San Jose, California

David C. Mann
St. Francis Hospital
Pittsburgh, Pennsylvania

Douglas L. Mann
V. A. Medical Center, Medical
  University of South Carolina
Charleston, South Carolina

Lester Mann
Hunter College, City University
  of New York
New York, New York

Donald S. Marozas
State University of New York
Geneseo, New York

Ellen B. Marriott
University of North Carolina
Wilmington, North Carolina

Tamara Martin
The University of Texas of the
  Permian Basin
Odessa, Texas

Patrick Mason
The Hughes Spalding International
  Adoption Evaluation Center
Georgia

Margo A. Mastropieri
Purdue University
Lafayette, Indiana

Deborah C. May
State University of New York
Albany, New York

Joan W. Mayfield
Baylor Pediatric Specialty Service
Dallas, Texas

Liliana Mayo
Centro Ann Sullivan
Peru

James K. McAfee
Pennsylvania State University
King of Prussia, Pennsylvania

Eileen F. McCarthy
University of Wisconsin
Madison, Wisconsin

Elizabeth McClellan
Council for Exceptional Children
Reston, Virginia

George McCloskey
The Psychological Corporation
San Antonio, Texas

Laura S. McCorkle
Texas A & M University
College Station, Texas

Linda McCormick
University of Hawaii, Manoa
Honolulu, Hawaii

Paul A. McDermott
University of Pennsylvania
Philadelphia, Pennsylvania

Phillip J. McLaughlin
University of Georgia
Athens, Georgia

James A. McLoughlin
University of Louisville
Louisville, Kentucky

Paolo Meazzini
University of Rome
Rome, Italy

Frederic J. Medway
University of South Carolina
Columbia, South Carolina

Brenda Melvin
New Hanover Regional
 Medical Center
Wilmington, North Carolina

James F. Merritt
University of North Carolina
Wilmington, North Carolina

Judith Meyers
San Diego, California

Danielle Michaux
Vrije Universiteit Brussel
Brussels, Belgium

Jennifer Might
University of North Carolina
Wilmington, North Carolina

Stephen Miles
Immune Deficiency Foundation
Towson, Maryland

James H. Miller
University of New Orleans
New Orleans, Louisiana

Ted L. Miler
University of Tennessee
Chattanooga, Tennessee

Norris Minick
Center for Psychosocial Studies
The Spencer Foundation
Chicago, Illinois

Anjali Misra
State University of New York
Potsdam, New York

Lisa Monda
Florida State University
Tallahassee, Florida

Linda Montgomery
The University of Texas of the
 Permian Basin
Odessa, Texas

Richard J. Morris
University of Arizona
Tucson, Arizona

Lonny W. Morrow
Northeast Missouri State University
Kirksville, Missouri

Sue Ann Morrow
EDGE, Inc.
Bradshaw, Michigan

Elias Mpofu
University of Zimbabwe
Harare, Zimbabwe

Tracy Muenz
California School of
 Professional Psychology
San Diego, California

Mary Murray
Journal of Special Education
Ben Salem, Pennsylvania

Jack Naglieri
Ohio State University
Columbus, Ohio

Sigamoney Naicker
Western Cape Educational
 SI Department
South Africa

Michael Nall
Louisville, Kentucky

Robert T. Nash
University of Wisconsin
Oshkosh, Wisconsin

Bonnie K. Nastasi
Kent State University
Kent, Ohio

Joyce Ness
Montgomery County
 Intermediate Unit
Norristown, Pennsylvania

Ulrika Nettelbladt
University of Lund
Sweden

Robert C. Nichols
State University of New York
Buffalo, New York

Etta Lee Nurick
Montgomery County
 Intermediate Unit
Norristown, Pennsylvania

Thomas Oakland
University of Florida
Gainesville, Florida

Festus E. Obiakor
Emporia State University
Nigeria

Masataka Ohta
Tokyo Gakujei University
Tokyo, Japan

John O'Neill
Hunter College, City University
 of New York
New York, New York

Alba Ortiz
University of Texas
Austin, Texas

Andrew Oseroff
Florida State University
Tallahassee, Florida

Lawrence J. O'Shea
University of Florida
Gainesville, Florida

Doris Paez
New Mexico State University
Las Cruces, New Mexico

Ellis B. Page
Duke University
Durham, North Carolina

Kathleen D. Paget
University of South Carolina
Columbia, South Carolina

Douglas J. Palmer
Texas A & M University
College Station, Texas

Hagop S. Pambookian
Elizabeth City, North Carolina

Ernest L. Pancsofar
University of Connecticut
Storrs, Connecticut

Sara Pankaskie
Florida State University
Tallahassee, Florida

Linda H. Parish
Texas A & M University
College Station, Texas

Daniel R. Paulson
University of Wisconsin at Stout
Menomonie, Wisconsin

Nils A. Pearson
Pro-Ed, Inc.
Austin, Texas

Mary Leon Peery
Texas A & M University
College Station, Texas

Olivier Périer
Université Libre de Bruxelles
Centre Comprendre et Parler
Brussels, Belgium

Joseph D. Perry
Kent State University
Kent, Ohio

Richard G. Peters
Ball State University
Muncie, Indiana

Faith L. Phillips
University of Oklahoma
    Health Science Center
Norman, Oklahoma

Jeffry L. Phillips
University of North Carolina
Wilmington, North Carolina

Yongxin Piao
Beijing Normal University
Beijing, China

Sip Jan Pijl
Gion University of Groningen
Groningen, The Netherlands

John J. Pikulski
University of Delaware
Newark, Delaware

Sally E. Pisarchick
Cuyahoga Special Education
    Service Center
Maple Heights, Ohio

Brenda M. Pope
New Hanover Memorial Hospital
Wilmington, North Carolina

John E. Porcella
Rhinebeck County School
Rhinebeck, New York

James A. Poteet
Ball State University
Muncie, Indiana

David P. Prasse
University of Wisconsin
Milwaukee, Wisconsin

Marianne Price
Montgomery County
    Intermediate Unit
Norristown, Pennsylvania

Elisabeth A. Prinz
Pennsylvania State University
University Park, Pennsylvania

Philip M. Prinz
Pennsylvania State University
University Park, Pennsylvania

Antonio E. Puente
University of North Carolina
Wilmington, North Carolina

Krista L. Puente
University of North Carolina
Wilmington, North Carolina

Nuri Puig
University of Oklahoma
Norman, Oklahoma

Craig T. Ramey
University of North Carolina
Chapel Hill, North Carolina

Sylvia Z. Ramirez
University of Texas
Austin, Texas

Arlene I. Rattan
Ball State University
Muncie, Indiana

Gurmal Rattan
Indiana University of Pennsylvania
Indiana, Pennsylvania

Anne Reber
Texas A & M University
College Station, Texas

Robert R. Reilley
Private Practice
Atlanta, Georgia

Fredricka K. Reisman
Drexel University
Philadelphia, Pennsylvania

Kimberly M. Rennie
Texas A & M University
College Station, Texas

Daniel J. Reschly
Vanderbilt University
Nashville, Tennessee

Cecil R. Reynolds
Texas A & M University
College Station, Texas

Robert Rhodes
New Mexico State Unviersity
Las Cruces, New Mexico

William S. Rholes
Texas A & M University
College Station, Texas

James R. Ricciuti
United States Office of
    Management and Budget
Washington, DC

Teresa K. Rice
Texas A & M University
College Station, Texas

Paul C. Richardson
Elwyn Institutes
Elwyn, Pennsylvania

Sylvia O. Richardson
University of South Florida
Tampa, Florida

Pamela Richman
University of North Carolina
Wilmington, North Carolina

Bert O. Richmond
University of Georgia
Athens, Georgia

Catherine Hall Rikhye
Hunter College, City University
of New York
New York, New York

Gary J. Robertson
American Guidance Service
Circle Pines, Minnesota

Kathleen Rodden-Nord
University of Oregon
Eugene, Oregon

Jean A. Rondal
Laboratory for Language,
Psychology, and Logopedics
University of Liege
Liege, Belgium

Sheldon Rosenberg
University of Illinois
Chicago, Illinois

Bruce P. Rosenthal
State University of New York
New York, New York

Kathy L. Ruhl
Pennsylvania State University
University Park, Pennsylvania

Joseph M. Russo
Hunter College, City University
of New York
New York, New York

Robert B. Rutherford, Jr.
Arizona State University
Tempe, Arizona

Anne Sabatino
Hudson, Wisconsin

David A. Sabatino
West Virginia College of
Graduate Studies
Institute, West Virginia

Lisa J. Sampson
Eastern Kentucky University
Richmond, Kentucky

Alfred Sander
Universitat des Saarlandes
Saarbruecken, Germany

Polly E. Sanderson
Research Triangle Institute
Research Triangle Park,
North Carolina

Scott W. Sautter
Peabody College, Vanderbilt
University
Nashville, Tennessee

Robert F. Sawicki
Lake Erie Institute of Rehabilitation
Lake Erie, Pennsylvania

Patrick J. Schloss
Pennsylvania State University
University Park, Pennsylvania

Ronald V. Schmelzer
Eastern Kentucky University
Richmond, Kentucky

Carol S. Schmitt
Eastern Kentucky University
Richmond, Kentucky

Sue A. Schmitt
University of Wisconsin at Stout
Menomonie, Wisconsin

Lyle F. Schoenfeldt
Texas A & M University
College Station, Texas

Eric Schopler
University of North Carolina
Chapel Hill, North Carolina

Fredrick Schrank
The Riverside Publishing Company
Itasca, Illinois

Louis Schwartz
Florida State University
Tallahassee, Florida

June Scobee
University of Houston, Clear Lake
Houston, Texas

Thomas E. Scruggs
Purdue University
Lafayette, Indiana

Denise M. Sedlak
United Way of Dunn County
Menomonie, Wisconsin

Robert A. Sedlak
University of Wisconsin at Stout
Menomonie, Wisconsin

John D. See
University of Wisconsin at Stout
Menomonie, Wisconsin

Sandra B. Sexton
Emory University School of Medicine
Atlanta, Georgia

Susan Shandelmier
Eastern Pennsylvania Special
Education Regional Resources
Center
King of Prussia, Pennsylvania

Alison Shaner
University of North Carolina
Wilmington, North Carolina

Deborah A. Shanley
Medgar Evers College, City
University of New York
New York, New York

William J. Shaw
University of Oklahoma
Norman, Oklahoma

Susan M. Sheridan
University of Wisconsin
Madison, Wisconsin

Naoji Shimizu
Tokyo Gakujei University
Tokyo, Japan

Ludmila Shipitsina
International University for
Family and Child
Russia

Edward Shirkey
New Mexico State University
Las Cruces, New Mexico

Dakum Shown
University of Jos
Nigeria

Lawrence J. Siegel
University of Texas Medical Branch
Galveston, Texas

Rosanne K. Silberman
Hunter College, City University
   of New York
New York, New York

Lissen Simonsen
University of North Carolina
Wilmington, North Carolina

Paul T. Sindelar
Florida State University
Tallahassee, Florida

Jerry L. Sloan
Wilmington Psychiatric Associates
Wilmington, North Carolina

Julie E. Smart
Utah State University
Logan, Utah

Craig D. Smith
Georgia College
Milledgeville, Georgia

Maureen A. Smith
Pennsylvania State University
University Park, Pennsylvania

Judy Smith-Davis
Counterpoint Communications
   Company
Reno, Nevada

Jane Sparks
University of North Carolina
Wilmington, North Carolina

Barbara S. Speer
Shaker Heights City School District
Shaker Heights, Ohio

Harrison C. Stanton
Private Practice
Las Vegas, Nevada

J. Todd Stephens
University of Wisconsin
Madison, Wisconsin

Cecelia Steppe-Jones
North Carolina Central University
Durham, North Carolina

Linda J. Stevens
University of Minnesota
Minneapolis, Minnesota

Rachael J. Stevenson
Bedford, Ohio

Mary E. Stinson
University of Alabama
University, Alabama

Roberta C. Stokes
Texas A & M University
College Station, Texas

Doretha McKnight Stone
University of North Carolina
Wilmington, North Carolina

Laura M. Stough
Texas A & M University
College Station, Texas

Michael L. Stowe
Texas A & M University
College Station, Texas

Edythe A. Strand
University of Wisconsin
Madison, Wisconsin

Elaine Stringer
University of North Carolina
Wilmington, North Carolina

Dorothy A. Strom
Ball State University
Indiana School of Medicine
Muncie, Indiana

Sheela Stuart
Georgia Washington University
Washington, DC

Sue Stubbs
Save the Children Fund
London, England

Kathryn A. Sullivan
Texas A & M University
College Station, Texas

Shelley Suntup
California School of
   Professional Psychology
San Diego, California

Emily G. Sutter
University of Houston, Clear Lake
Houston, Texas

Mark E. Swerdlik
Illinois State University
Normal, Illinois

Henri B. Szliwowski
Hôpital Erasme, Université Libre
   de Bruxelles
Brussels, Belgium

Pearl E. Tait
Florida State University
Tallahassee, Florida

Paula Tallal
University of California
San Diego, California

Mary K. Tallent
Texas Tech University
Lubbock, Texas

C. Mildred Tashman
College of St. Rose
Albany, New York

James W. Tawney
Pennsylvania State University
University Park, Pennsylvania

Ellen A. Teelucksingh
University of Minnesota
Minneapolis, Minnesota

Cathy F. Telzrow
Kent State University
Kent, Ohio

Spencer Thompson
The University of Texas of the
   Permian Basin
Odessa, Texas

Steven R. Timmermans
Mary Free Bed Hospital and
   Rehabilitation Center
Grand Rapids, Michigan

Gerald Tindal
University of Oregon
Eugene, Oregon

Francine Tomkins
University of Cincinnati
Cincinnati, Ohio

Carol Tomlinson-Keasey
University of California
Riverside, California

Bruce Thompson
Texas A & M University
College Station, Texas

Raymond Toraille
Public Education
Paris, France

Jose Luis Torres
Texas A & M University
College Station, Texas

Stanley O. Trent
University of Virginia
Charlottesville, Virginia

Timothy L. Turco
Louisiana State University
Baton Rouge, Louisiana

Lori E. Unruh
Eastern Kentucky University
Richmond, Kentucky

Cynthia Vail
Florida State University
Tallahassee, Florida

Greg Valcante
University of Florida
Tallahassee, Florida

Hubert B. Vance
East Tennessee State University
Johnson City, Tennessee

Aryan Van Der Leij
Free University
Amsterdam, The Netherlands

K. Sandra Vanta
Cleveland Public Shools
Cleveland, Ohio

Don Viglione
California School of
    Professional Psychology
San Diego, California

Judith K. Voress
Pro-Ed, Inc.
Austin, Texas

Emily Wahlen
Hunter College, City University
    of New York
New York, New York

Deborah Klein Walker
Harvard University
Cambridge, Massachusetts

Donna Wallace
The University of Texas of the
    Permian Basin
Odessa, Texas

Raoul Wallenberg
International University for
    Family and Child
Russia

Marjorie E. Ward
The Ohio State University
Columbus, Ohio

Sue Allen Warren
Boston University
Boston, Massachusetts

John Wasserman
The Riverside Publishing Company
Itasca, Illinois

Lauren Webster
University of North Carolina
Wilmington, North Carolina

Danny Wedding
Marshall University
Huntington, Virginia

Frederick F. Weiner
Pennsylvania State University
University Park, Pennsylvania

Marjorie Weintraub
Montgomery County
    Intermediate Unit
Norristown, Pennylvania

Bahr Weiss
University of North Carolina
Chapel Hill, North Carolina

Shirley Parker Wells
University of North Carolina
Wilmington, North Carolina

Louise H. Werth
Florida State University
Tallahassee, Florida

Catherine Wetzburger
Université Libre de Bruxelles
Brussels, Belgium

Larry J. Wheeler
Southwest Texas State University
San Marcos, Texas

Susie Whitman
Immune Deficiency Foundation
Towson, Maryland

Thomas M. Whitten
Florida State University
Tallahassee, Florida

J. Lee Wiederholt
Pro-Ed, Inc.
Austin, Texas

Saul B. Wilen
Medical Horizons Unlimited
San Antonio, Texas

Greta N. Wilkening
Children's Hospital
Denver, Colorado

Mary Clare Williams
Ramey, Pennsylvania

Diane J. Willis
University of Oklahoma Health
Sciences Center
Oklahoma City, Oklahoma

Victor L. Willson
Texas A & M University
College Station, Texas

John D. Wilson
Elwyn Institutes
Elwyn, Pennsylvania

Margo E. Wilson
Lexington, Kentucky

Joseph C. Witt
Louisiana State University
Baton Rouge, Louisiana

Bencie Woll
University of Bristol
Bristol, England

Bernice Y. L.Wong
Simon Fraser University
Buraby, British Columbia

Mary M. Wood
University of Georgia
Athens, Georgia

Diane E. Woods
World Rehabilitation Fund
New York, New York

Frances F. Worchel
Florida State University
Tallahassee, Florida

Eleanor Boyd Wright
University of North Carolina
Wilmington, North Carolina

Logan Wright
University of Oklahoma
Norman, Oklahoma

Karen F. Wyche
Hunter College, City University
of New York
New York, New York

Martha Ellen Wynne
Loyola University of Chicago
Chicago, Illinois

James E. Ysseldyke
University of Minnesota
Minneapolis, Minnesota

Roland K. Yoshida
Fordham University
New York, New York

Thomas Zane
Johns Hopkins University
Baltimore, Maryland

Lonnie K. Zeltzer
University of Texas Health
Science Center
San Antonio, Texas

Paul M. Zeltzer
University of Texas Health
Science Center
San Antonio, Texas

Kenneth A. Zych
Walter Reed Army Medical Center
Washington, DC

FOREWORD

After Cecil Reynolds and Elaine Fletcher-Janzen asked me to write the foreword for the second edition of the *Encyclopedia of Special Education,* I reread the original foreword, which was written in 1987 by Samuel A. Kirk. Dr. Kirk is regarded by most professionals as the "Father of Special Education," and I had the honor of working with him at the University of Arizona. I share his strong feelings about the value of special education and this encyclopedia. Although Dr. Kirk is deceased, the ideas he expressed in the original foreword are still true; thus I chose to retain most of his original text in this edition.

The creation of the *Encyclopedia of Special Education* represented the coming of age for a field of endeavor that not so many years ago drew little public interest or concern, both in society at large and within education in particular. Those of us who served in special education during its earlier years, when public commitment to its needs was minimal or even lacking, cannot help but be pleased with, and astonished at, the vast enterprise it has now become.

Special education has developed very gradually over the past 160 years. From approximately 1850 to 1900, the care, management, and education of children with disabilities was conducted primarily in facilities sponsored by religious organizations or in residential institutions for the deaf, the blind, the mentally deficient, and the delinquent. From 1900 to approximately 1950, public schools in large cities began to educate both gifted children and a small percentage of children with disabilities. After 1950, some states began providing subsidies to local public schools to encourage the establishment of special education and to decrease the demands made on overcrowded and dilapidated state residential schools. During this period, the federal government offered no financial assistance to the states, believing that education was a state responsibility and that federal aid would lead to federal control of education.

Later in the decade, the precedent of denying federal aid was discarded. Parents began to organize and demand services and funding for their children with disabilities— not just at the state level, but at the federal level as well. President Eisenhower responded by asking Congress to provide assistance, and Congress appropriated several million dollars to be used for research and for the preparation of professional personnel.

The major expansion and social revolution within special education came in the 1960s during the administration of John F. Kennedy, who dispatched task forces to various countries to survey their programs for children with disabilities. After hearing the task force reports, he presented Congress with a comprehensive research and training bill, the Mental Retardation Facilities and Community Mental Health Centers Construction Act of 1963, which was followed by a number of congressional acts that encompassed many different kinds of services. In 1975, Congress enacted P.L. 94-142, The Education for All Handicapped Children Act. Interestingly, the wording of this act follows the language of the United States Declaration of Independence. It has been paraphrased as follows:

> We hold these truths to be self-evident, that all children, handicapped and nonhandicapped, are created equal; that they are endowed by their creator with certain inalienable rights, among these are the right to equal education to the maximum of each child's capability. To secure these rights, Public Law 94-142 was established. We, the people of these United States, solemnly declare that all exceptional children shall be educated at public expense, and that their education will be in the least restrictive environment. (Kirk & Gallagher, *Educating Exceptional Children,* 3rd ed. 1979, xi)

During the following years, Congress and US presidents continued to pass legislation and provide additional funds to states, universities, colleges, and local education agencies. The most recent legislation—the Individuals with Disabilities Education Act Amendments of 1997 (P.L. 105-17), signed by President Clinton—recognized that most students with disabilities now spend most or all of their time in general education classrooms. Provisions included in these amendments specified that general education teachers participate in the creation of Individual Education Programs (IEPs) for students identified with disabilities.

It is particularly gratifying to see that a major public commitment has been made to special education for students with exceptionalities in the United States and throughout much of the world. This is true not only in Canada and western Europe (where achievements in many areas of special education service often preceded and inspired those in the United States) but also in Japan, Indonesia, and other less advanced and less affluent parts of the globe, all of which are represented in this encyclopedia. Worldwide, concerned professionals and parents have sought to provide for the education of children and youth with disabilities, often in spite of extremely limited resources.

This growth in special education, and the extraordinary commitment of financial and human resources to service and research over the past two decades, has meant an explosion of information scattered throughout a wide variety of journals and books. Thus, even with all the advances in media technology, professionals find it very difficult to obtain the information they need. Despite the contributions of abstracting services, databases, reviews, and handbooks to managing the special education knowledge base, coherent control and accessibility are still issues for professionals in related fields and interested lay persons.

The original *Encyclopedia of Special Education* was designed to present a comprehensive picture of special education in a readily understandable, usable, and summative form. The editors have successfully updated and expanded the award-winning first edition while continuing to preserve the original goals of clarity and completeness. By using it, individuals seeking special education information are able to understand both the broad scope of the field and also the detailed areas of endeavor within it. Comprehensive yet succinct, the *Encyclopedia* literally provides an A

to Z examination of special education. Furthermore, it does so through well-written explanations devoid of unnecessary detail. The *Encyclopedia* offers a scope and view of special education not readily obtained from other sources. In addition, the issuance of this second edition comes at a most propitious time, because special education has now taken innovative directions that are likely to continue well into the next century.

This work has become an essential reference tool, not only for professionals in special education, but also for lawyers, physicians, psychologists, social workers, school board members, and others who assist in or formulate policies for the education of individuals with disabilities and gifted persons. Its ultimate usefulness may be in its utility for the lay person, however: When all is said and done, it is informed citizens who are the guardians of special education. The *Encyclopedia of Special Education* has found a niche in many libraries—public, college, and professional. Dr. Cecil Reynolds and Dr. Elaine Fletcher-Janzen and their consulting editors should be congratulated for taking the time and effort to compile this gargantuan encyclopedia.

J. LEE WIEDERHOLT, EdD
President, Donald D. Hammill Foundation

PREFACE TO SECOND EDITION

The first edition of the *Encyclopedia of Special Education* was originally conceived to be a primary reference for many disciplines and professionals concerned with both the education of exceptional children and their special characteristics, needs, and problems. It was hoped that the *Encyclopedia* would serve as a desktop reference containing essential information for educators, psychologists, physicians, social workers, lawyers, ministers, and occupational, physical, and speech therapists. The *Encyclopedia* was also intended to be used by lay persons such as parents of exceptional children, school board members, advocates of handicapped persons, legislators, and other concerned individuals seeking to be more knowledgeable about the education of exceptional children.

The latter description turned out to be exactly how the *Encyclopedia* has been used over the past decade. There is always a need for a place to start researching a topic at hand and always a need for an in-depth reference point. The *Encyclopedia* entries were designed to define a subject, relate the history of the subject, explain the research and treatment of the subject in an objective manner, and relate the body of knowledge to everyday special education practices. This format hopefully leaves the reader with a solid overview of the subject and how research translates into practice. The references at the end of each entry help the reader explore the basis for the entry and direct the reader to further research. As with the first edition, the use of technical language was maintained at a minimum to maximize the readability of the text.

There are over two thousand entries in the second edition. They can be categorized much the same as the first edition: biographies, educational and psychological tests, interventions and service delivery, handicapping conditions, related services, legal, and miscellaneous. The miscellaneous grouping of entries has grown in the second edition, probably due to the addition of many more entries on subjects such as rare or orphan diseases, internet resources, and cultural perspectives on different subjects.

The number of staff members and contributors for the second edition is considerably smaller than that of the first edition. This was intentional. The first edition used over 400 authors, and even with the expertise of a large board of contributing and consulting editors, there was some redundancy and inconsistency in writing level and style. The board of consulting editors for the second edition consisted of seven individuals with extensive experience in both the field of special education and related fields. The consulting editors had considerably fewer authors writing for them. In addition, approximately half of the second edition was updated by the volume editors themselves. All in all, this arrangement changed the flow of the second edition into a tight, quality-controlled format.

As with the first edition, we hope that the *Encyclopedia* will serve in many functions:

1. a source of basic, summative information
2. a basic spot reference
3. a textbook
4. a continuing information-support system.

The second edition has changed, obviously, to reflect the times and preparation for the next century. Our experience of editing the first and second editions has given us a unique perspective on how special education has grown in the past fifteen years: A chance to look back and see what plans came to fruition, what promises were kept, and what developments were unforeseen. The following are some reflections on how the second edition is different in substance from the first edition:

1) Cultural competence: It is now mandatory that individuals involved in special education have training in cultural awareness and are working on the process of becoming culturally competent. This includes all special education (and regular education) personnel and materials. The terms "multicultural" and "minority" have been replaced with "culturally and linguistically diverse." This change reflects the huge increases in the Spanish-speaking school population and the recognition that "ethnicity" and "culture" are not synonymous terms. Cultural awareness does not denote competency; therefore, teacher training programs have included more than cursory introductions to working with diverse students and curricula. School psychologists can no longer receive certification and licensure that do not include competency in evaluating, developing, and interpreting tests that are culturally sensitive. Legislation and regulations about special education continue to ad-

dress cultural issues of long standing such as the underrepresentation of ethnic minorities in gifted programs and the overrepresentation of ethnic minorities in programming for mental retardation and behavior disorders, and newer issues such as the implementation of part H of the Individuals with Disabilities Education Act and culturally appropriate familial partnerships. The school population is changing rapidly, and special education is reflecting an appreciation of the diversity in a meaningful way.

2) Service delivery: The continuum of service delivery in special education has changed considerably in the past fifteen years. The first edition of the *Encyclopedia* discussed Deno's Cascade of Services and mainstreaming, and the second edition covers the evolution of the Regular Education Initiative into the Inclusion movement. As with all new ideas, there are extremists who insist on full inclusion for all special education students, extremists who refuse to embrace inclusion at all, and the moderate majority who are beginning to connect the individualistic nosology of recent IDEA amendments with including special education students based on the least restrictive placement mandate. Our only cause for concern with the Inclusion movement, however well-intentioned, is that it was brought about and put into operation in the public schools without pilot projects or the benefit of objective scientific evidence. Good ideas and moral thoughts are not enough for the basis of a revolution in service delivery. We hope that serious mistakes were not made with the education of so many children by good intentions. As we speak, there is still a scarcity of well-controlled studies to document the effectiveness of inclusion. This is somewhat ironic while another major change in special education is in full swing: the call for accountability.

3) Accountability: Accountability of programs has been another new movement in the 1990s. Federal legislation calls for accountability and, therefore, assessments of special education students focus on outcome. The field is no longer interested in the material that goes into the teaching process: Special education is interested in measuring student performance. Curriculum-based assessment and other alternative assessments are popular and indicative of this movement, but also fail to meet the test of research to back up their intuitively appealing claims.

4) Expansion of services: Special education services have expanded considerably since the first edition. Part H of IDEA spells out a considerable program of services for infants and toddlers, and Part B supports the three- to five-year-old students and their transition into kindergarten. All of these services must now actively involve the parents and/or family of the child to ensure support and generalization across settings.

5) The internet: The impact of the World Wide Web on special education has been considerable. The number of well-controlled and designed web sites that disseminate information about handicapping conditions, organizations, medical information, interactive groups, and research continues to grow. The average special education teacher or parent of an exceptional child can gain support and information about virtually any topic related to special education. Indeed, most special educators can now write an Individual Education Plan on a template and paste or insert objectives from extensive state or federal databases into the document. In fact, most special education files are computerized, which has led to a set of guidelines for handling electronic documentation. The dissemination of information from web sites such as the U.S. Department of Education, Deaf World Web, Educational Administration, and databases such as ERIC means that information is current and interactive. Such sources are powerful tools for special education.

There have been other salient events in the field as well. There have been many foreign adoptions in the past fifteen years, especially from eastern Europe. It has given us the opportunity to study the results of early deprivation in new ways. Unfortunately, the results of deprivation are faced by adoptive parents in the United States, who become all too aware of the sequelae of deprivation and the special education services needed to assist. The field is finding out more and more about rare diseases and databases on them are being developed. The growth of the internet has helped the spread of information about rare diseases, and has helped many families and professionals needing discourse.

James Flynn and others are tying to figure out why IQs have been increasing consistently for the past several decades. Different theories are being posed, such as improvements in nutrition, test sophistication, and cultural complexity. The debate on these phenomena will surely continue and be very interesting.

Attention-deficit/hyperactivity disorder has gained a place in the Other Health Impaired category of exceptionality. The incidence and prevalence of this disorder has caused much research and concern.

Traumatic Brain Injury (TBI) has gained its own place in an eligibility category for special services. The unique needs of TBI students were recognized legislatively in the 1990s. Unfortunately, the advent of managed care involvement in the restriction of services for TBI students means that TBI patients are often discharged from rehabilitation hospitals prematurely and left to seek out ad hoc services locally. Further, this means that school systems are encountering TBI students much earlier in their recovery and are far less prepared to manage the complex demands of TBI recovery.

Technology for the handicapped is currently in its heyday. Apart from access to the internet, software companies have revolutionized access to information and expression for the deaf, blind, and individuals with multiple handicaps. This accessibility has increased communication within exceptionalities and has contributed to the solidarity of deaf culture, blind athletes, and many more.

In terms of format for the second edition, for all entries that were written by the consulting editors and their teams, the first edition entry author's name was kept at the end of each entry. The second edition's author placed his or her name with the first edition author if the entry was just updated. Of course, if the entry needed complete revision, the second edition author name was placed by itself. For all of the other entries, we updated them ourselves. All entries that only have the first edition's author name at the end were reviewed and additions and deletions were made accordingly by the volume editors. We apologize to our first edition authors if we changed the intent of their work for the second edition. However, it was important that all work in this text be current and applicable to today's special education.

Over 200 entries in the second edition are completely new. Approximately 5 percent of the first edition entries were deleted because they were obsolete or redundant. Nearly 700 entries were updated or rewritten by the consulting editors and their teams. Over 300 biographies, journals, and organizations were updated and approximately 120 "See" entries were reviewed for better cross-referencing. The second edition, although not seminal, was still a massive project and therefore requires our thanks to many individuals. We would like to thank our contributing editors:

Bob Brown (University of North Carolina–Wilmington) for his experience in editing and for his breadth and depth of knowledge in the field of special education. Bob's entries for the first edition were superb and the culmination of his years of experience, insight, and humanism is evident in these volumes.

Jan Hasbrouck and Rich Parker (Texas A&M University) for their coverage of culturally and linguistically diverse and international students. This perspective is central to the updating of the *Encyclopedia* and is well represented.

Donald Hammill (Pro-Ed, Inc.) undertook the task of updating and reviewing many new tests and special education materials.

Kay Ketzenberger (University of Texas of the Permian Basin) took on the pursuit of biographees, journal editors, and organizations who had moved or changed their names. Her detective work is legendary!

Liz Lichtenberger (The Salk Institute) tackled the evaluation of many, many current tests and assessment instruments. As an editor, determining which tests were to be deleted, deemed historical, added, and evaluated was a formidable job indeed.

Robert Rhodes (New Mexico State University) gave his editorial perspective on the Speech/Language entries in the *Encyclopedia*. Robert's clarity of thought and organization were truly soothing in the chaos!

Of course, we offer many thanks to all of the authors of both first and second editions for their scholarly contributions and dedication to the field of special education.

There are other individuals who contributed to the *Encyclopedia* one entry at a time. We would like to thank Susie Whitman for her entry on Primary Immune Deficiency Disorder. This entry is the beginning of many articles that Susie will write during her career as a chronic illness counselor and as the mother of Amy, who has bravely managed Primary Immune Deficiency since birth. Krista Biernath, another contributor, is a physician spearheading research about post-institutionalized children at Emory University.

We must also thank Jennifer Simon for her guidance through the knotty problems that come up from time to time. Problems tend to snowball in a work of this size, and Jennifer kept us on the right path.

We do not get tired of thanking our families for their support during our hours away on our never-ending projects. Elaine would like to thank David, Emma, Leif, Win, and Peter for their tolerance and humor during the last mile of the project, especially when the computer blew up(!). Cecil continues to be appreciative of Julia for her support, tolerance, and guidance through the many briar patches of life he seems destined to discover!

We hope the second edition of the *Encyclopedia of Special Education* is of service to the many individuals in the field who help exceptional children. There have been many changes in the field over the past fifteen years, but some things will always stay the same: There are exceptional children and there are individuals with good will who wish to help them.

CECIL R. REYNOLDS
Texas A&M University

ELAINE FLETCHER-JANZEN
University of Northern Colorado

PREFACE TO FIRST EDITION

Exceptional children, i.e., handicapped or gifted individuals between the ages of birth and 23, constitute (depending on various types of estimation) nearly 10% of children and adolescents who receive educational services throughout the world. The field of endeavor concerned with this education is generally designated as special education.

Special education is a broad domain encompassing many different concerns and types of children. There long has been a need for a publication that provides ready access to authoritative and comprehensive, yet current and succinct, information about this category of education and its many related aspects. The *Encyclopedia of Special Education* is just such a publication. It is intended as a primary reference for many disciplines and professions concerned with the education of exceptional children and with their special characteristics, needs, and problems. The *Encyclopedia* will continue to serve for many years as a desktop reference containing essential information for educators, psychologists, physicians, social workers, occupational and physical therapists, lawyers, and ministers.

The *Encyclopedia of Special Education* is, however, more than just a professional reference book. It also is intended for use by intelligent lay people, including parents, school board members, advocates of handicapped persons' rights, legislators, and concerned citizens seeking to be more knowledgeable about the education of exceptional children. Indeed, as Raymond J. Corsini, editor of the *Encyclopedia of Psychology* (1984) (Wiley-Interscience) wrote in his preface to that valuable reference work, it can be argued that "professionals [themselves] are lay people when not reading in their own specialized field." It was on this basis that he sought to make his encyclopedia "understandable to the average intelligent layperson (Corsini, p. xxi). It is on this basis, too, that we have prepared the *Encyclopedia of Special Education* as a source of authentic and authoritative information expressed with clarity and conciseness. Though technical language is used, the level of presentation was carefully reviewed to achieve this goal of utility and readability.

The preparation of the *Encyclopedia of Special Education* presented many challenges. Among the foremost was the fact that over the past two decades or so, the needs and rights of exceptional children have moved from a position of relative obscurity and neglect to a position in the center of public consciousness and obligation to a degree unanticipated and even inconceivable in earlier generations.

Originally, special education was a small, poorly understood, and underfunded field that attempted to meet the needs of but a few children, first under the rubric of "the education of exceptional children" and then, in recent years, under that of "special education." Over the course of several decades, special education has become a massive multidimensional movement involving many different groups and interests and making important claims on public attention and funding. Thus, the *Encyclopedia of Special Education* has a broad scope. Though it is primarily concerned with the education and training of gifted and handicapped children, it also extends into psychology, medicine, and politics, to mention but a few of the noneducational fields. The inclusion of these fields is critical to an appreciation of special education. Indeed, the *Encyclopedia of Special Education* attempts to touch on all areas and fields deemed relevant to an understanding of what late twentieth century and early twenty-first century special education is about.

The volumes each follow a traditional encyclopedic structure and are organized alphabetically. Each topic is covered succinctly, giving the most crucial information and directing the reader to more extensive treatments of the issues. There are more than two thousand included in the work. Although presented alphabetically, the various entries can be grouped conceptually into seven major categories.

1. *Biographies*—brief descriptions of key figures in the field, both living and deceased, and their key contributions to special education.

2. *Educational and psychological tests*—brief descriptions and commentary on tests with applications to special education are provided, but more extensive discussions are given of tests with widespread use or with a particularly complex structure. Tests are given under their proper titles and not by acronyms or popular titles. Acronyms are indexed and cross-referenced in most cases for ease of locating information.

3. *Interventions and service delivery*—techniques of intervention and the delivery of special education services to individuals are discussed and reviewed.

4. *Handicapping conditions*—conditions that require special education services are described.

5. *Related services*—services necessary to support the effectiveness of special education but not usually deemed to be special education services per se are described and their relevance to special education noted.

6. *Legal*—major court cases, legislation, and legal concepts related to the field of special education are noted and their implications for special education are reviewed.

7. *Miscellaneous entries*—this category includes special education topics that are not classified under the previous categories but that are substantive and relevant to the field (e.g., measurement terms, prevention projects, major works, journals, professional associations, and terms such as epidemiology, school psychology, vocational counselor, naturalistic observation, and effectiveness of special education).

These categories were derived primarily for the use of editors, consulting editors, and the publisher's staff. However, they are valuable to the users of the *Encyclopedia* as well as they help to locate items of interest. To address such a diverse array of topics and to maintain a balanced view on what can be a controversial field, two groups of advisers were formed: the Board of Consulting Editors, who had important writing and supervisory responsibilities shared with the editors, and the Editorial Advisory Board, professionals who advised the editors, did limited writing, and provided specialty reviewing for a variety of topics. These individuals were chosen to represent a host of theoretical positions, areas of expertise, disciplines (special education, psychology, medicine, speech pathology, physical therapy, educational psychology, and school psychology, to name a few), demographic and ethnic characteristics, and national origins. Practitioners, academicians, administrators, and others are represented here as well. Experts from many disciplines of science, education, politics, and philosophy contributed to the *Encyclopedia*. Each author is credited with a byline at the end of each entry. Those entries listed as authored by Staff were prepared by Elaine Fletcher-Janzen, E. Valerie Hewitt, Angela Baily, and Cecil Reynolds, with the assistance of various sources. Many of these entries are biographies in which the staff was assisted by the biographees. All living biographees were asked to review their entries for factual accuracy; most were extremely helpful and cooperative in this regard.

A great challenge in the creation of the *Encyclopedia of Special Education* was the recognition that special education is a worldwide concern rather than a concern narrowly defined and interpreted in terms of events proceeding within the boundaries of the United States. Fortunately, the *Encyclopedia* was able to draw on the expertise of authorities familiar with the international aspects of special education to assist in providing access to information worldwide about developments relevant to special education.

Still another challenge to the *Encyclopedia of Special Education* was to respond to the historical antecedents and roots of special education as well as to current issues. A significant effort, and a successful one was to ensure that the *Encyclopedia* would provide its users with succinct, pertinent information relative to the foundations of special education in addition to information bearing on its immediate concerns.

Indeed, the *Encyclopedia of Special Education* has gone to great lengths to give all of the aspects of special education their due. It is hoped that the *Encyclopedia* will serve as an efficient and effective aide for practitioners, scientists, parents, and intelligent laypersons alike, and for many years to come. We have been helped in this task by the expert opinions and advice of authorities across a broad range of disciplines. Recommendations for topics to be included in the *Encyclopedia* and opinions about those topics were sought from many experts, going far beyond even the insightful comments of our consulting editors and Editorial Advisory Board. Indexes of all major works in the field were examined, computer searches were conducted, and practitioners in special education were asked their opinion. Reference librarians throughout the United States were consulted. As preparation of the *Encyclopedia* proceeded, further topics were solicited and prepared as late as 2 weeks prior to the publisher's final deadline for submission. Inevitably, something will be missing and we, the editors, accept full responsibility for any such sins of omission.

As a consequence of the broad diversity of sources for the topics suggested, the *Encyclopedia* is an ecumenical work, a manifestation of many divergent streams of thought brought together in a flow of convergent achievement. There are more than 380 contributors all concerned, though often in quite different ways, with the education, training, and management of exceptional individuals. Users of the *Encyclopedia of Special Education* will find that it serves a variety of purposes. The *Encyclopedia* serves the profession and the public:

1. *As a source of basic summative information.* Users of the Encyclopedia of Special Education will find it valuable first and foremost as an immediate source of concise summative information about special education, rehabilitation, and childhood exceptionality; it covers topics in these areas literally from A to Z. The *Encyclopedia*'s information is presented in ways that make it very accessible. Readers seeking information will find it available in quick and easy to comprehend form, whether the information they seek concerns definitions or concepts, theories or histori-

cal personages, critical assessment techniques, issues of intervention techniques employed in special education, laws and regulations, or key projects and key persons. Great effort was made to ensure that the *Encyclopedia*'s entries are as contemporary as possible. In many instances, the *Encyclopedia*'s users will find the information offered on most topics to be sufficient for their purposes. When more extensive information is required, the *Encyclopedia* will guide its users to other sources of information both through cross-references within the *Encyclopedia* itself and to other texts as well.

2. *As a basic spot reference.* A most important use of the *Encyclopedia of Special Education* is to serve as a source for spot references. Using its entries or its extensive index, the user can look up and check out particular topics for names, definitions, and the like. The user can identify other topics related to a particular area and learn quickly how to access them. The *Encyclopedia* is more useful, in many ways, than abstracts or abstract services for tracking down information.

3. *As a textbook.* The *Encyclopedia* is not intended to serve as a primary text for a basic or core course in childhood exceptionality or special education. However, it will serve as a useful supplementary text for almost any course at either undergraduate or graduate levels, serving to amplify the topics in such courses or to extend the knowledge networks of concepts, practices, and research. The *Encyclopedia* also can serve as a primary text for advanced courses or seminars; as such, the student will be left with a set of books that will serve him or her long into a professional career. The *Encyclopedia* also should be helpful to students and scholars who need a concise yet precise guide to information in education, psychology, etc., for review purposes, either for comprehensives or licensure or certification. Graduate students approaching comprehensive exams should find the work useful, especially on their reference shelves as they move ahead toward the practice of special education.

4. *As a continuing information-support system.* Well beyond the immediate needs of knowledge and information, the *Encyclopedia of Special Education* will serve as a source of continuing education for its owners. Regular, even review of its contents will ensure its readers of a deeper understanding relative to special education and related fields. In professional and public libraries, it will serve as a network control system permitting the management of other resources concerning the education of exceptional children.

A project as massive as the *Encyclopedia* requires the joint work of an inordinate number of individuals. To our authors we must offer our first round of thanks. They worked in a timely manner, jovially revising their first efforts in many cases and under tight editorial guidelines. Our Editorial Advisory Board gave excellent advice in reviewing, writing, and generally advising at various stages of the project. All are listed in the front matter. The Board of Consulting Editors gave a yeoman's effort in all cases. Each consulting editor had significant supervisory and writing responsibilities; without their help we would still be struggling.

Many others desrve our thanks. Joan Kappus gave hours and hours to the development of the master list of entries. E. Valerie Hewitt began working with us only during the last 6 months of manuscript preparation, but was a godsend nevertheless. Mike Ash, Head of the Department of Educational Psychology at Texas A&M University, was instrumental in obtaining the university support necessary for such a large project. Mike's support, moral and professional, and as a friend, was necessary and welcomed—and very typical of this extraordinary department head. The Research Assistance Laboratory of the College of Education at Texas A&M University, under the direction of Victor Willson, graciously gave us cherished space for housing the *Encyclopedia* office and operations. Hugh J. Scott, dean of the Division of Programs in Education at Hunter College, provided an encouragement of scholarship in special education that was inspirational and deserving of our appreciation.

Angela Bailey was our administrative editor and was responsible for coordinating all aspects of the day-to-day operations of the office. She corresponded with hundreds of authors, cajoled the tardy, smoothed ruffled feathers, and served as chief operations officer, making everyone adhere to schedule, the editors included. She handled all with humor, aplomb, and efficiency. We could not have done it without her and consider ourselves fortunate to have had the insight to have hired her.

Elaine Fletcher-Janzen, senior editorial associate, read and edited every piece of manuscript for content and for style. She coordinated writing assignments and consistently performed well beyond the expected. Elaine prepared background material for more entries than any individual author and prepared her own entries, while also coordinating the review process. Elaine is truly the proverbial gem. She is the kind of graduate assistant and doctoral student that we came to academia hoping to mentor; we hope she has learned as much from us as we have learned from her while she progressed through her doctoral studies—and all while starting her family—another successful venture we are sure.

The overall guidance of the work can be ascribed to Dr. Martin Grayson, editor of the Encyclopedia Division of John Wiley & Sons. Martin believed in us and the project from the beginning. A journal and an encyclopedia editor as well as a scholar in his own field, Martin gave essential guidance, urging us on through inspiration as well as an occasional shove when our labors flagged. The staff of production editors at Wiley was most helpful as well, consistent with our experience with a half dozen other Wiley projects. In particular, Cary Weinberger and her predecessor April Kelliher deserve recognition for their coordination from the publisher's office. Margery Carazzone, Production Manager and Rosalind Greenberg, Production Editor, performed superbly.

To our families, our friends, and our secretaries, we needed your patience and understanding as we struggled to meet deadlines and asked more than we should have from you. You so graciously accommodated us. Thank you. And, Julia, thanks for the crucial times of sanity you bring to a very crazy life. CRR would like to express a special note of appreciation to his mentors, Alan S. Kaufman and E. Paul Torrance, who continue to inspire. To the users of the *Encyclopedia,* we await your comments on this work and hope that you will find it helpful to you in helping children grow and develop to the utmost of their potential.

CECIL R. REYNOLDS
LESTER MANN

College Station, Texas
New York, New York
April 1987

Encyclopedia of
SPECIAL
EDUCATION
Second Edition

A

AAAS

See AMERICAN ASSOCIATION FOR THE ADVANCEMENT OF SCIENCE.

AAMD CLASSIFICATION SYSTEMS

The American Association on Mental Deficiency (AAMD) was founded in 1876 to support and promote the general welfare of people who are mentally retarded through professional programs, dissemination of research and program advances, and development of standards for services and facilities. The organization is comprised of approximately 10,000 professionals from many different disciplines who are concerned with the prevention and treatment of mental retardation. The association publishes two research journals, *Mental Retardation* and *American Journal of Mental Deficiency*. A national conference, along with many regional and state conferences, is held each year to give professionals the opportunity to share significant information regarding the education and welfare of children and adults with mental retardation.

The first diagnostic and classification system was published in 1921. It was reviewed and revised in 1933, 1941, 1957, 1959, 1973, 1977, and 1983. In each case, the manual was revised based on new developments in philosophy and knowledge of the field. To make the revisions and clarify important issues, input is culled from presentations at national and regional meetings of the AAMD, national and local hearings, and discussions with representatives of many professional, social, and political action groups. All revisions are made by the AAMD's Terminology and Classification Committee after a careful examination of the present classification system and the new data. Major revisions over the years have centered around the presentation of a dual classification system, medical and behavioral; clarification of the definitions of adaptive and measured intelligence; the addition of an extensive glossary; an illustration of levels of adaptive behavior; and procedures for diagnosing mental retardation in the behavioral system. With this last example, it is important that clinicians understand, in diagnosing mental retardation, the concept of standard error of measurement and its use in making a clinical determination of retardation and level of functioning.

The 1983 AAMD classification system developed by the AAMD's Terminology and Classification Committee has been written to reflect current thinking in the field. This latest edition has three distinct purposes. First, the 1983 edition was an attempt to provide an acceptable system to be used worldwide. It was developed in coordination with the International Classification of Diseases-9 (ICD-9) of the World Health Organization, the American Psychiatric Association's *Diagnostic and Statistical Manual-III* (DSM-III), and the American Association on Mental Deficiency's Classification in Mental Retardation.

The second purpose was to improve opportunities to gather and disseminate information regarding diagnosis, treatment, and research activities. The third purpose of this classification system was to provide opportunities for the identification of causes of mental retardation with implications for prevention.

The definition of mental retardation accepted by most authorities is the one used by the American Association on Mental Deficiency. The definition was presented first by Heber in 1961 and later revised by Grossman in 1973 to read: "Mental retardation refers to significantly subaverage general intellectual functioning resulting in or associated with concurrent impairments in adaptive behavior and manifested during the developmental period." Based on the definition, to be classified mentally retarded, the person must be below average in both measured intelligence and adaptive behavior.

The AAMD classification of the retarded has been useful to professionals as well because it is based on the severity of retardation. The terms used by the AAMD are mild, moderate, severe, and profound.

The AAMD causal classification scheme centers around nine general groupings for mental retardation. These groups include infections and intoxication, trauma or physical agent, metabolism or nutrition, gross brain disease, unknown prenatal influence, chromosomal anomalies, other conditions originating in the perinatal period following psychiatric disorder, and environmental influences.

REFERENCES

Grossman, H. (Ed.). (1983). *Classification in mental retardation.* Washington, DC: American Association on Mental Deficiency.

CECELIA STEPPE-JONES
North Carolina Central University

AAMD ADAPTIVE BEHAVIOR SCALES MENTAL RETARDATION

AAMR ADAPTIVE BEHAVIOR SCALES–RESIDENTIAL AND COMMUNITY: SECOND EDITION (ABS–RC:2)

The *AAMR Adaptive Behavior Scales–Residential and Community: Second Edition* (ABS–RC:2) (Nihira, Leland, & Lambert, 1993) is the revision of the 1969 and 1974 *AAMD Adaptive Behavior Scales.* The latest version of the adaptive behavior scales is the product of a comprehensive review of the earlier versions of the rating scales relating to persons with mental retardation in the United States and other countries. The items of the ABS–RC:2 have undergone numerous modifications since the 1969 edition as a result of intensive item analyses over time, with different group results varying with respect to adaptive behavior levels. The scale items that survived this process were selected on the bases of their inter-rater reliability and their effectiveness in discriminating (a) among institutionalized persons with mental retardation and those in community settings who previously had been classified at different adaptive behavior levels according to the AAMD's Classification in Mental Retardation (Grossman, 1983) and (b) among adaptive behavior levels in public school populations. This scale is appropriate for individuals from ages 18 through 80.

Domain raw scores are converted to standard scores (M = 10, SD = 3) and percentiles. Factor raw scores are used to generate quotients (M = 100, SD = 15) and percentiles. The scale's normative sample consists of more than 4,000 persons from 43 states with developmental disabilities residing in the community or in residential settings. The test has been extensively examined regarding reliability and validity, and the evidence supporting the scale's technical adequacy is provided in the manual. Internal consistency reliabilities and stability for all scores exceed .8.

This scale was reviewed in *The Thirteenth Mental Measurements Yearbook* (Impara & Plake, 1998) by Carey (1998) and Harrison (1998). Carey stated that the scale is technically adequate for this type of assessment; Harrison

reported that the ABS–RC:2 has many features that enhance the assessment of adults with developmental disabilities.

REFERENCES

Carey, K. T. (1998). Review of the AAMR Adaptive Behavior Scale–Residential and Community, Second Edition. In J. C. Impara & B. S. Plake (Eds.), *The thirteenth mental measurements yearbook* (pp. 3–5). Lincoln: Buros Institute of Mental Measurements, University of Nebraska Press.

Grossman, H. J. (Ed.). (1983). *Classification in mental retardation.* Washington, DC.: American Association on Mental Deficiency (now Retardation).

Harrison, P. L. (1998). Review of the AAMR Adaptive Behavior Scale–Residential and Community, Second Edition. In J. C. Impara & B. S. Plake (Eds.), *The thirteenth mental measurements yearbook.* Lincoln: Buros Institute of Mental Measurements, University of Nebraska Press.

Impara, J. C., & Plake B. S. (Eds.). (1998). *The thirteenth mental measurements yearbook* (pp. 1–3). Lincoln: Buros Institute of Mental Measurements, University of Nebraska Press.

Nihira, K., Leland, H., & Lambert, N. (1993). *AAMR Adaptive Behavior Scales–Residential and Community: Second Edition.* Austin, TX: Pro-Ed.

TADDY MADDOX
Associate Director of Research, PRO-ED, Inc.

AAMR ADAPTIVE BEHAVIOR SCALES–SCHOOL: SECOND EDITION (ABS–S:2)

The *AAMR Adaptive Behavior Scales–School: Second Edition* (ABS–S:2) (Lambert, Nihira, & Leland, 1993) is used for assessing the current adaptive functioning of children being evaluated for evidence of mental retardation, for evaluating adaptive behavior characteristics of children with autism, and for differentiating children with behavior disorders who require special education assistance. The scale is appropriate for children ages 3 years to 18 years 11 months.

This revision is divided into two parts. Part One focuses on personal independence; it is designed to evaluate coping skills considered important to independence and responsibility in daily living. The skills within Part One are grouped into nine behavior domains: Independent Functioning, Physical Development, Economic Activity, Language Development, Numbers and Time, Prevocational/Vocational Activity, Self-Direction, Responsibility, and Socialization. Part Two measures socially maladaptive behaviors. The behaviors assessed were identified through a survey of the social expectations placed upon persons with mental retardation in public and special schools, public and private residential institutions, and a wide range of local rehabilitative and recreational services. The descriptions of those expectations were obtained from an analysis of a large number of critical incident reports provided by personnel in residential, community, and school settings. The behaviors in Part Two are assigned to seven domains, which are measures of those adaptive behaviors that relate to the manifestation of personality and behavior disorders: Social Behavior, Conformity, Trustworthiness, Stereotyped and Hyperactive Behavior, Self-Abusive Behavior, Social Engagement, and Disturbing Interpersonal Behavior. The domains in Part One and Part Two are combined into five factors: Personal Self-Sufficiency, Community Self-Sufficiency, Personal-Social Responsibility, Social Adjustment, and Personal Adjustment.

Domain raw scores are converted to standard scores (M = 10, SD = 3) and percentiles. Factor raw scores are used to generate quotients (M = 100, SD = 15) and percentiles. The scale's normative sample consists of more than 2,000 persons from 31 states with developmental disabilities attending public schools and more than 1,000 students who have no disabilities. The test has been examined extensively regarding reliability and validity. Internal consistency reliabilities and stability for all scores exceed .8.

In *The Thirteenth Mental Measurements Yearbook*, Stinnett (1998) reviewed the instrument and concluded that the scale's psychometric qualities are good; Harrington (1998) stated that the ABS–S:2 makes a contribution to the area of adaptive behavior assessment. Both reviewers felt the test was improved from previous editions.

REFERENCES

Harrington, R. G. (1998). Review of the AAMR Adaptive Behavior Scale–School, Second Edition. In J. C. Impara & B. S. Plake (Eds.), *The thirteenth mental measurements yearbook* (pp. 5–9). Lincoln: Buros Institute of Mental Measurements, University of Nebraska Press.

Lambert, N., Nihira, K., & Leland, H. (1993). *AAMR Adaptive Behavior Scales–School: Second Edition*. Austin, TX: PRO-ED.

Stinnett, T. A. (1998). Review of the AAMR Adaptive Behavior Scale–School, Second Edition. In J. C. Impara & B. S. Plake (Eds.), *The thirteenth mental measurements yearbook* (pp. 9–14). Lincoln: Buros Institute of Mental Measurements, University of Nebraska Press.

TADDY MADDOX
*Associate Director of Research,
Pro-Ed, Inc.*

AAMD CLASSIFICATION SYSTEMS
ADAPTIVE BEHAVIOR

ABAB DESIGN

The ABAB design is one of the oldest and most widely used single-case designs developed in behavioral psychology. It was initially used in laboratory studies with animals (Sidman, 1960); however, as the applied behavior analysis movement got under way (Baer, Wolf, & Risley, 1968), it became a prototype for applied behavioral investigations conducted in the natural environment. Although the number of single-case designs has increased markedly since the early days of applied behavior analysis (e.g., Kazdin, 1980; Kratochwill, 1978), the ABAB design still occupies a prominent place in applied behavioral research. Moreover, because of the high degree of experimental control that it provides, it has been widely used with individuals manifesting various types of handicaps (Bergan, 1977). For example, the ABAB design has been particularly useful in studying environmental variables affecting language acquisition in retarded children (Bergan, 1977).

The ABAB design is intended to reveal a functional relationship between an experimental treatment and a behavior targeted for change. For example, it might be used to establish a functional relationship between the use of the plural form of a noun and a treatment such as praise following the occurrence of a plural noun. The demonstration of a functional relationship between praise and plural nouns would require an association between the frequency of plural-noun production and the occurrence of verbal praise. Given that a functional relationship were established, verbal praise could be assumed to function as a positive reinforcer increasing the probability of occurrence of plural nouns by the subject or subjects participating in the experiment.

The ABAB technique has often been referred to as a single-case design (e.g., Kratochwill, 1978). However, it may be applied with more than one subject. Thus, the term single case is a bit misleading. Glass, Wilson, and Gottman (1975) among others called attention to the fact that the ABAB design is a time-series design in that it reflects an effort to determine changes in behavior occurring across a series of points in time. Recognition of the ABAB design as a time-series design opened the way for linking the design to the statistical procedures associated with time-series analysis (see, for example, Glass, Wilson, & Gottman, 1975). Application of time-series analysis procedures affords a statistical test for hypotheses that may be investigated with the ABAB design. However, despite this advantage, time-series techniques have not been widely used in applied investigations involving the ABAB design. There are a variety of reasons for this. Among them is the fact that the graphing techniques suggested by behavioral psychologists (e.g., Parsonson & Baer, 1978) as an alternative to statistical analysis are easier to implement and to interpret than time-series statistics. Nonetheless, time-series procedures constitute a potentially powerful tool for applied behavioral research and their use can be expected to increase in the future.

As the letters in its name suggest, the ABAB design includes four phases. The initial A phase is a baseline period that records behavior across a series of points in time in the absence of intervention. The length of the baseline period varies depending on the variability of the behavior being recorded. If the behavior is highly variable, a longer baseline is required than if the behavior is highly stable. More data are required to get a sense of the fluctuations that may be expected without intervention for a highly variable behavior than for a highly stable behavior. The second phase, denoted by the letter B, is a treatment phase. During this phase the treatment is introduced. The treatment may be implemented in accordance with a variety of different schedules. For example, treatment may be implemented with every occurrence of the target behavior. For instance, praise might be given following every occurrence of a plural noun. On the other hand, treatment might be implemented in accordance with one of the many available partial reinforcement schedules. Thus, praise might be given after every third occurrence of a plural noun. The third phase, also denoted by the letter A, constitutes a return to baseline. The return to baseline may be brought about by various means. One is to withdraw the treatment. For instance, praise might not be given following plural-noun utterances during the return-to-baseline phase. Another procedure is to introduce another treatment intended to bring the target behavior back to baseline level. For example, reinforcement of a behavior that is incompatible with the target behavior may be introduced during the return-to-baseline phase. The final phase in the ABAB design, denoted by the second occurrence of the letter B, is a second implementation of the treatment. The second implementation is intended to demonstrate treatment control over the target behavior by minimizing the possibility that environmental influences occurring coincidentally with the treatment could be responsible for the observed behavior change.

The major advantage of the ABAB design lies in the fact that it minimizes the likelihood of coincidental environmental influences on the target behavior. There are two potential disadvantages to the approach (Kazdin, 1973). One is that some behaviors are not easily reversed. For example, a skill that has been well-learned may not be easy to unlearn. The second disadvantage is that there are cases in which it may not be practical to carry out a return-to-baseline even if it is possible to do so. For instance, a teacher may not want to return a child's performance of an academic skill to baseline even for a short period of time. Despite these shortcomings, the ABAB design has been shown to be useful in establishing a functional relationship between a treatment and behavior in countless appli-

cations. It is truly a mainstay in applied behavioral research and will continue to be used widely.

REFERENCES

Baer, D. M., Wolf, M. M., & Risley, T. R. (1968). Some current dimensions of applied behavior analysis. *Journal of Applied Behavior Analysis, 8,* 387–398.

Bergan, J. R. (1977). *Behavioral consultation.* Columbus, OH: Merrill.

Glass, G. V., Wilson, V. L., & Gottman, J. M. (1975). *Design and analysis of time-series experiments.* Boulder: Colorado Associated University Press.

Kazdin, A. E. (1973). Methodological and assessment considerations in evaluating reinforcement programs in applied settings. *Journal of Applied Behavior Analysis, 6,* 517–531.

Kazdin, A. E. (1980). *Research design in clinical psychology.* New York: Harper & Row.

Kratochwill, T. R. (1978). *Single-subject research: Strategies for evaluating change.* New York: Academic.

Parsonson, B. S., & Baer, D. M. (1978). The analysis and presentation of graphic data. In T. R. Kratochwill (Ed.), *Single-subject research: Strategies for evaluating change.* New York: Academic.

Sidman, M. (1960). *Tactics of scientific research.* New York: Basic.

JOHN R. BERGAN
University of Arizona

RESEARCH IN SPECIAL EDUCATION

ABECEDARIAN PROJECT

For the past quarter century, American education has been especially concerned with the academic performance of children from disadvantaged families. This special concern stems from the well-established fact that this group of children typically performs well below average on standardized tests of academic achievement. They also are overrepresented in special education classes. The root causes of this poor performance are not well understood but their consequences are costly, in terms both of economics and psychological dysfunction. Such consequences have frequently been called developmental retardation.

To ameliorate these costly consequences, a wide variety of special education programs have been investigated under the rubric of compensatory education. Most of these programs have concentrated on the so-called preschool and/or early elementary school years. The primary hypothesis has been that educational experiences that augment and/or supplement the educational experiences of the home will better prepare disadvantaged children for academic accomplishment in the public schools. The Abecedarian project has been such an experiment. Abecedarian means one learning the rudiments of something (the alphabet).

The specific aims of the Abecedarian project have been:

To determine whether developmental retardation and school failure can be prevented in children from socially and economically high-risk families by means of educational day care.

To determine whether a follow-through program for early elementary school is necessary to maintain preschool intellectual gains in high-risk children.

To determine whether school-age intervention alone can significantly improve academic and/or intellectual performance in children who did not have preschool intervention.

To identify a sample of families at high risk for having a developmentally retarded child, a high-risk screening index (Ramey & Smith, 1977) was developed. This index included social, environmental, and psychological factors judged on the basis of the developmental literature to be associated with poor intellectual and scholastic progress. Each factor was assigned a weight based on professional consensus as to its likely importance in determining intellectual and scholastic outcomes. Thirteen factors were included; among them were paternal and maternal education; family income; father's absence; retardation among other family members; family disorganization; maladaptive or antisocial behavior within the family; and unstable job history.

Based on the high-risk index, families were judged to be at elevated risk and eligible for inclusion in the study. Characteristics of the 109 families (111 children) eventually enrolled in the study are given in the following Table. As may be seen in the Table, the families in the sample were predominantly black (98%), were headed by a single female (72%) who was young (20 years) and who had less than a high school education (10.23 years).

It is a special feature of the Abecedarian project that participants were assigned to the preschool experimental educational treatment or control condition at random. Fifty-seven children were randomly assigned to the preschool experimental group, 54 were preschool controls. Ninety-six children remained in the study to be randomly assigned to a school-age treatment group.

At public school entry, Abecedarian children within the two preschool groups were rank-ordered according to 48-month Stanford-Binet IQ's; each consecutive pair was randomly assigned to the school-age experimental or control groups. All families accepted their school-age assignment, but three children assigned to the preschool control-school-

Entry Level Demographic Data for Experimental and Control Families

Experimental Variable	Group		
	Control (N = 55)	Experimental (N = 54)	Total (N = 109)
1. Mean high risk index	20.08 (5.72)	21.41 (5.88)	20.75 (5.81)
2. Mean maternal age (years)	19.62 (3.87)	20.28 (5.77)	19.94 (4.89)
3. Mean maternal education (years)	10.46 (1.75)	10.00 (1.89)	10.23 (1.83)
4. Mean maternal IQ (WAIS full scale)	85.49 (12.34)	84.18 (10.78)	84.84 (11.61)
5. Percent female-headed family	78%	65%	72%
6. Percent black families	96%	100%	98%

age experimental condition (CE) moved away and did not participate in the school-age phase.

Figure 1 gives the overall design of the Abecedarian study, including the preschool and school-age treatment programs and the number of children randomly assigned to each condition. The Abecedarian study can be conceptualized as a 2×2 factorial design. The factors are preschool educational treatment versus no preschool treatment and school-age educational treatment versus no school-age treatment. Thus, there were two preschool groups, the experimental (E) and control (C) groups, and four school-age conditions: preschool experimental school-age experimental (EE); preschool experimental school-age control (EC); preschool control school-age experimental (CE); and preschool control school-age control (CC). These groups varied in the intensity (defined as number of years) of intervention: 8 years for the EE group; 5 years for the EC group; 3 years for the CE group; none for the CC group.

The preschool program may be characterized as a comprehensive, whole child program. The aim was to create a rich, stimulating, yet orderly environment in which the children could grow and learn. The curriculum was designed to enhance cognitive and linguistic development and to provide the children with many opportunities for successful mastery experiences. The curriculum materials

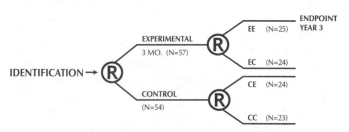

Figure 1. Research design of Carolina Abecedarian Project.

included those for infants and preschoolers developed by Sparling and Lewis (1979). In addition, there was an enriched language environment that was responsive to the children's needs and interests (Ramey, et al., 1982).

In many ways the program was not unlike other high-quality infant daycare and preschool programs. Child/caregiver ratios ranged from 1:3 for infants to 1:6 for four year olds. Teachers typically had early childhood education experience and participated in an extensive in-service education program. The children's experiences became increasingly more structured over the preschool years, eventually coming to include prephonics programs and science and math experiences in addition to an emphasis on language and linguistic development. The presumption was that when the child left the preschool, he or she would be able to enter kindergarten without experiencing an abrupt transition.

Children attended the preschool program beginning between 6 weeks and 3 months of age. Children attended the daycare program 5 days per week, 50 weeks per year. The center was open from 7:30 A.M. to 5:15 P.M. Free transportation to and from the center was provided for families who needed it. Almost all of the children were transported by center staff. This portion of the program has been described in more detail by Ramey, MacPhee, and Yeates (1982).

The school-age intervention program began in kindergarten. It consisted of providing a home/school resource teacher to each child and family in the two Abecedarian school-age experimental groups (EE and CE) shown in Figure 1. These teachers filled many roles: they were curriculum developers who prepared an individualized set of home activities to supplement the school's basic curriculum in reading and math; they taught parents how to use these activities with their children; they tutored children directly; they met regularly with classroom teachers to ensure that home activities matched the skills being taught in the classroom; they served as consultants for the classroom teacher when problems arose; and they advocated for the child and family within the school and community. Thus, they facilitated communication between teacher and parent, providing an important support for disadvantaged parents who frequently lacked the skills and confidence needed to advocate for their children within the school system, an institution seen by many as both monolithic and difficult to comprehend. Each home/school resource teacher had a caseload of approximately 12 families per year. The home/school resource teachers were experienced educators familiar with the local school system.

The supplemental curriculum delivered as home activities concentrated on two basic subjects: reading and math. These subjects were emphasized because it seemed likely that high-risk children might need extra reinforcement of these basic concepts to master and to remember them. The program sought to provide such reinforcement, presuming

that scholastic performance would best be enhanced by direct teaching and practice of needed basic skills. The curriculum packets contained teaching activities that parents and children could share and enjoy. In addition, work sheets to give extra drill and practice were often included.

Home/school teachers made approximately 17 school visits per year for each child. During these visits they met with the classroom teacher to identify the skills currently being taught and to learn which areas needed extra work or review. A variety of specialists within the system were contacted, including special education resource personnel, reading teachers, and school counselors. Efforts were made to coordinate the child's program and to make sure the best available resources were being used.

The home component of the program was equally intense. Home visits were made about 15 times each school year. A typical visit lasted approximately 30 to 45 minutes, with the mother being the most likely participant. Teachers reviewed the classroom situation and showed the parent the materials in the activity packet, explaining the purpose and directions for each activity. The child was present and participated in about one-quarter of the home visits; this was often helpful because it allowed the teacher to demonstrate how an activity was to be carried out. Parents reported spending an average of 15 minutes a day working with their children on home activities. Parent response to the activities was very positive; very few reported that they failed to use the activities although direct verification was not possible.

Many forces other than intellectual ability and encouragement to learn can have an impact on a child's scholastic performance: emotional upset within the home, parental unemployment, the death of a family member, or instability of living arrangements, to name a few. Home/school resource teachers sometimes helped families deal with personal crises. Extra home visits occurred if and when the home/school teacher attempted to help the family solve such real-life problems. Home/school teachers also helped to provide the children with a variety of summer experiences, including summer activity packets, summer camp, trips to the public library, and, for some children, a six-week tutorial in reading.

The results to be included here cover the intellectual and academic outcomes for Abecedarian children through the first 2 years in public school. Many other results are available, but these have been chosen because they represent the primary outcome hypotheses under investigation.

Figure 2 gives the IQ results for Abecedarian children from infancy through age 6½ years (78 months). In Figure 2, the mean IQs are graphed by preschool group up to the age of 60 months and by the four school-age groups thereafter. The scores are Bayley Mental Developmental Indices at 3, 6, 9, 12, and 18 months, Binet IQs at 24, 36, and 48 months, and full-scale IQs on the Wechsler Preschool and Primary Scale of Intelligence at 60 months and the Wech-

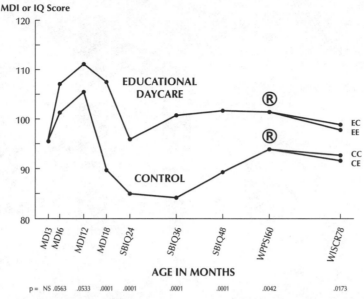

Figure 2. Mean mental development (MDI's) and IQ scores for randomly assigned high-risk children from 3 to 78 months of age in the Abecedarian Project.

sler Intelligence Scale for Children-Revised at 78 months.

The preschool intervention had a positive effect on intellectual development of the high-risk children in the experimental group, as may be seen in Figure 2. Throughout the preschool period, at every testing occasion after 12 months, significant mean differences on standardized test scores werc found between the two Abecedarian preschool groups (Ramey & Campbell, 1984). The primary form of this effect was to reduce the drop in mental test scores evidenced by the control group. It is now apparent that this preschool effect persists up through 78 months (Ramey &

Campbell, in press). There is no evidence, however, that the school-age intervention significantly impacted children's intellectual performance during the first year and half of public school. No significant effect of the school-age program was found at 78 months. Thus regardless of school-age intervention status, the two groups who had preschool intervention maintained their relative superiority in tested intelligence over children who were preschool controls.

Figure 3 from Ramey and Campbell (in press) contains the kindergarten and first grade Peabody Individual

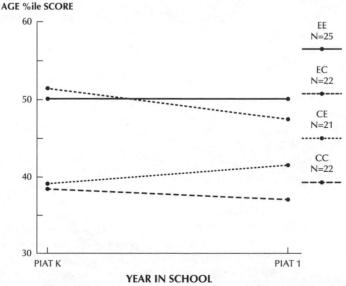

Figure 3. Mean age-referenced percentile scores on the Peabody Individual Achievement Test by year in school for the groups in the Abecedarian Project.

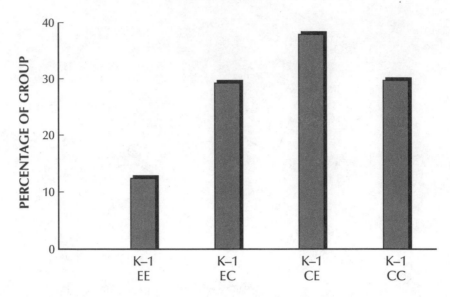

Figure 4. Percentage of high-risk children retained in grades as a function of experimental educational conditions.

Achievement Test results in terms of age-referenced percentile scores. Examination of this figure reveals that the preschool groups are near national average whereas the preschool control groups are below national average. Thus during the first 2 years in public school, positive preschool treatment effects on academic achievement were observed.

Figure 4 presents the percentage of children retained in either kindergarten or first grade for each of the four experimental conditions. One-eighth, or 12%, of the children in the EE group were retained in grade during the first 2 years of public school, compared with approximately one-third in the other three groups. Although it is very early in these children's public school careers, it is remarkable that the academic failure rate is so high in the groups that did not receive early and continuing supplemental education. The one-third grade retention rate is clearly costly and apparently reducible through intensive early education. Such a high retention rate also buttresses the initial judgment that these children were indeed at elevated risk for school failure.

Together, the data on IQs, academic achievement, and retention in grade suggest that preschool intervention exerts a positive influence on intelligence and school success in the first 2 years of public school. Preschool intervention supplemented by continued help in the early grades via a home/school resource teacher program shows promise for being the most effective intervention. This intensity of effort apparently enabled the high-risk children in this sample to maintain a level of achievement near the national average. In addition, the likelihood of being retained in grade was less by a factor of approximately three for children who had early and continued educational intervention.

We are currently in the process of analyzing data for the final year of the school-age intervention. When those analyses are completed and we have systematically examined the family, school, and child factors associated with academic performance, we hope to have a better understanding of the forces that are associated with the academic performance of children from disadvantaged families and the ability of educational intervention to ameliorate those forces.

REFERENCES

Ramey, C. T., & Campbell, F. A. (1984). Preventive education for high-risk children: Cognitive consequences of the Carolina Abecedarian project [Special issue]. *American Journal of Mental Deficiency, 88*(5), 515–523.

Ramey, C. T., & Campbell, F. A. (in press). The Carolina Abecedarian project: An educational experiment concerning human malleability. In J. J. Gallagher (Ed.), *The malleability of children.* Baltimore, MD: Brookes.

Ramey, C. T., MacPhee, D., & Yeates, K. O. (1982). Preventing developmental retardation: A general systems model. In L. A. Bond & J. M. Joffe (Eds.), *Facilitating infant and early childhood development* (pp. 343–401). Hanover, NH: University Press of New England.

Ramey, C. T., McGinness, G. D., Cross, L., Collier, A. M., & Barrie-Blackley, S. (1982). The Abecedarian approach to social competence: Cognitive and linguistic intervention for disadvantaged preschoolers. In K. Borman (Ed.), *The social life of children in a changing society.* Hillsdale, NJ: Erlbaum.

Ramey, C. T., & Smith, B. (1977). Assessing the intellectual consequences of early intervention with high-risk infants. *American Journal of Mental Deficiency, 81,* 318–324.